SMILE BECAUSE IT HAPPENED

FOREWARD

A few years ago, Dad thought it would be a great idea to buy mom an IPAD for Christmas. Well, along with the dog, the IPAD quickly became his.

When he began the grueling process of dialysis 2 years ago, he also learned how to operate the IPAD, and it became his friend during those long hours of being hooked to that machine. During this time, he took on a project of writing his life story. Well, I have to tell you, it wasn't easy. Dad would call and let me know that he spent hours writing and then would accidentally delete his work or something. I'm sure it had to be difficult, especially since his vision was so bad. I just can't imagine typing on an IPAD with it 2 inches from my face while hooked up to a dialysis machine. But Dad did it. He could do anything.

He had asked if I could put his book together for him and I was proud to do so. For 2 years during dialysis, Dad would email me the stories that he had typed that day. As I look back now on all of the emails I received, I am still amazed how he was able to type, especially without being able to see well at all and, in the end, seeing only with one eye.

The morning of his operation, he told Mom and I that he had made his last entry and finished the book. Here it is. I promise you that I only corrected typos. As you read, I'm sure you will feel his love, humor and presence as I do.

Jane

JAMES PASS MELSON

Born: February 26, 1935   **Died:** May 23, 2013

I was born at the Delaware County Hospital to Anna Pass Melson and Walter Francis Melson. This is a story of my life as best as I can remember it. I want my grandchildren to know who I was and how I lived my life.

I had one older brother, Walter Francis Melson, Jr. nicknamed Mel. He was born November 30, 1926 and died March 27, 2002, age 76. I had two older sisters, Marlene who was born in 1931 and died in 1935 and Marie Jane Melson who was born May 3, 1933 and died April 21, 2007, age 74.

We lived with my Dad's Mom and Dad on City Line Avenue, about 2 miles west of West Chester Pike on their 40 acre farm in Drexel Hill, Philadelphia. We lived on the 3rd floor until my Dad designed and built a house next door on the farm. He also designed and built my Grandparents house. I was still in diapers when we moved to Solebury, at the corner of Sugan Road, Route 263 and Phillips Mill Road. My

Dad built our house on Phillips Mill Road and called it Watercress Springs. Some of my nicknames were Bowie, Bo, Bimmy and Mel.

I do not remember this but the story goes that one day I was still in diapers and could only crawl. I crawled out the door into the center of Route 263 and sat in the middle of the road. We had a German Sheppard named Wings. Well Wings came out and sat next to me. A state dump truck came along and realized what was going on. He stopped and went to get out but Wings wouldn't let him out of the truck so he sat there and kept blowing his horn until Mom came out to see what was going on and rescued me. I must have gotten my but spanked. Mom sent the story into **Don McNeal's Breakfast Club.** It was a radio program in the morning that everyone listened to and Wings won a year of dog food for saving my life. It was the only time that the dog had anything to do with me but that was O.K. It was enough.

When I was about 9 or 10, I liked to take things apart. My Grandfather had an old wind up alarm clock for me to take apart. Of course putting them back together was another thing. One time my Dad bought a reel type power lawn mower made by

Firestone. I mean nobody had a power mower in those days. Well I took it all apart trying to see how it worked. My Dad was not happy about it and had to take it to a lawn mower shop to have it put back together.

I liked to mow grass and increased the size of our lawn quite a bit. I mounted 2 flashlights on the mower so I could mow at night when it was cooler out. Sometimes I would mow until 10:00 at night. We had the best looking lawn in the neighborhood.

My Grandparents had a 40 acre farm on City Line Avenue in Drexel Hill. They grew all kinds of stuff. They had 2 horses that worked the farm and 3 farm help (men that lived in the basement). They got room and board. Mike, Tony and Bill. They were of Polish or Russian descent. When my Grandmother died, my Mom and my sister and I moved to their farm to keep house and cook for the men. I went to the 5th grade down there that year. When Pop Pop died, we moved back to our farm, bringing the men with us. One time my brother had a BB gun. It was all I could do to crank it and I took it into our kitchen where the men were eating lunch. I told Mike to look down the barrel. When he did I pulled the trigger, hitting him in the eyebrow. Boy did I get my ass beat then. Mike did not stay working with us very long so we had Tony and Bill until they died. Bill died first and I guess Tony got very lonely without him and hung himself in our basement. Then we had no help.

We used to supply all of the chives to Sylvan Seal in Philadelphia which Bill always went all around cutting chives. Somehow Mom hired a guy by the name of Harry Eichlin (Bud) and he kept us supplied with chives. Little did I know that he would become my Father in Law one day.

The year I lived at Pop Pop's he grew a lot of mountain pink so I set up a little roadside stand. I made enough money to pay all of the help that month.

As a boy, I loved to make model airplanes and hang them from the ceiling of my bedroom. I joined the New Hope Model Club. The club was run by my Dad, Mr. Marc Walton, Mr. Nat Forbes and Mr. Sam Bodine. We had about 12 members including Jim Smoyer, Leon Clark, Dick Shuck, George Bennett, Dick Skid, Jim Shoenthal, my sister and brother. We flew gas powered planes on 50 ft. wires, called U

Control. You could do all kinds of stunts with them. In 1947-1948, the New Hope Exchange Club had a model meet held at the New Hope Solebury High School. It was a big deal. Kids came from all over to compete. They had all kinds of prizes. One summer I worked and saved enough to buy a McCoy engine. It cost 75 bucks. I built a speed plane and the first time I flew it, it did 102 mph. We also had a ram jet engine that started by using a bike pump. It was very loud.

As I grew older, I loved to hunt and trap. Having all of those watercress beds was heaven and full of muskrats. I had about 75 traps and I had to get up at 5:00 in the morning to check them before school. I would get 4 or 5 a day and got $1.50 to $4 a rat, depending on how big they were. I made a lot of money for a kid.

The first time I was allowed to go hunting I was 10 years old. You had to be 12 to get a license so all I could use was a BB gun. Naturally I didn't get anything. When I was finally old enough I used to hunt everyday with my dog, Lindy. One day I asked my Dad for a new box of shotgun shells. He asked me how many I had left so I told him I had 5 shells. He said "well, see what you get". When I returned that afternoon I had 2 pheasants and 3 rabbits. Needless to say I was very proud of myself and I got a new box of shells.

I lived about 2 miles from school so I would hunt to school, unload my shotgun and put it into the coat closet. You could do that in those days. My bus driver always had a loaded rifle on the bus during deer season. They always closed school for the first day of hunting. When I was about 13, my Dad took me deer hunting. I was using a colt lightning cal 32-20 pump rifle. It held 13 bullets. Well, believe it or not I bagged a 6 point buck, it dressed out at 152 lbs. I hit it with my first shot and then I got what they called buck fever. The deer ran off but I could not stop shooting at the spot where I first saw it. I shot 13 times and then reloaded 4 more shells and fired them at the empty spot. My Dad showed me how to track the deer and I found it about half of a mile away. It was quite an experience.

As I grew older, I got interested in cars. My sister had a Model A Ford, 2 door sedan. Of course growing up on a farm, I learned to drive when I was about 14, driving tractors and trucks. My best friend and neighbor, Jim Smoyer who is 3 years older than me had his driver's license and sometimes Mom would let me have the car as long as Jimmy would do the driving. Well as soon as we got out of our driveway, I would take over. I used to drive all over the place and never got caught.

About that time, my Mom and Dad got a divorce. He took off to Florida and left us with about $40,000 in debt. It was hard. My sister got a job as a companion and driver for an elderly couple. I got a job washing cars for Wes Hendricks gas station in Stockton, NJ. I also worked for Dick Havens on his farm. My Mom took a job as a companion for Mrs. Mattlack and had to live at her house, leaving my sister and I at home by ourselves. Mel was married and had his own family to take care of.

As hard as we tried, we were not able to pay off the debt so we had a sheriff's sale. Pete Pazziso who owned the quarry bought everything, the house, and cars and then gave it back to us. He had a good heart. It was very embarrassing but we hung on. Mom was able to quit her job and moved back home. We had 2 men that lived in our basement (farm help). They worked for my grandparents and then for my folks most of their lives. Tony and Bill. Tony was from Poland and Bill was from Russia. He was in the Russian army and only had one eye. Tony got $15 per week and Bill got $10 per week plus room and board. They became part of our family.

As I said, I worked for Dick Havens on his farm. He was my brother's best friend. They had the same kind of car and you could not tell them apart. The day I turned 16, he took me to Philadelphia for my driver's test and I passed. That night I drove a load of watercress to the dock street in New York City. I made out O.K. until on the way home, I had a little fender bender. They built a new drive-in movie theater at Ringoes and this old lady was sitting in the middle of the road watching the movie and I guess I was watching it too. Well I hit her right in the ass. It wasn't too bad and it was still drivable. I was afraid to go home and tell Mom but I did and it was O.K.

HIGH SCHOOL YEARS

My first car was a Model A Ford roadster with a V8 motor. It was a real hot rod. It had no top and one tail light but when you stepped on the brake I had 32 stop lights that came on. I painted dotted lines around the doors with a sign saying OPEN HERE! I payed 40 bucks for it. My next car was a 1939 Ford 2door sedan and it burnt oil like mad so I decided to rebuild the engine. I had some problems but a mechanic at the quarry told me how to do it. When I went to start it the car would not turn over. I had the bearings too tight and I didn't oil them when I installed them. Mel and Havey pushed me up to Tony Shucks garage in Stockton. He said to leave it so I did. Later I found out that he got his son Dick to push it with the wrecker and got it going to about 60 mph, popped the clutch, it started and ran great.

Most of the guys in my class had cars. All of them were Fords so we had what we called FORD ALLEY and would park them in a line at the school parking lot. We would park them about half an inch apart so you had to climb out the window to get out. We thought we were pretty cool.

I guess we all raised a lot of hell with our loud mufflers, flame throwers and auto bombers and drag racing. The state cops started sitting in front of the high school so for 4 days we all hid our cars behind the gym and rode the buses until the cops left. A couple of weeks later they did stop me and looked under the car. Either they didn't see the spark plug in my tail pipes or didn't know what they were, but they let me go. There was one guy during his senior year bought and sold 35 cars. He was a real used car salesman.

We would all drive our cars loaded with kids to the soccer away games. Of course we would always race both ways. It's a wonder some of us weren't killed. The school did not provide any buses for them. What a blast we used to have. Sometimes we would switch drivers while doing 60 or 70 mph. It was called "rotation". We did some pretty dumb things back then. One night I pushed Carl Otte over the New Hope river bridge at 60 mph. The bridge cop never caught us. You never knew when one of your buddies would sneak up behind you and just start pushing your car.

Jimmy Smoyer and I would ride our bikes to Lambertville and go to the movies. The matinee. It was 2 miles from home. Sometimes we would buy a pack of cigarettes and smoke the whole pack before we got home.

Another thing we used to do on summer nights was to fill a box with chicken shit and gift wrap it with a bow and everything. Then we would set it in the middle of the road and hide in the bushes and wait for a car to stop and pick it up. It was great fun. One night we got a long pole, picked up a dead skunk and put it in a guy's mailbox. Another time we borrowed some sawhorses and some detour signs and set them up at a guy's driveway. He could not figure out why all these cars were turning around in his driveway all night long.

One of the things that we did in jr. high school was to paint our shoes. One might be red and yellow and the other would be blue and green. My folks did not push me in school and so I took the easiest courses that I could. My favorite was math and shop and study hall. We would have a lot of dances where the kids would actually dance. We would have bands and decorate the gym. One time we had Eddie Fisher. I guess he was just starting out. I could not play any sports because I had to work at home. The favorite saying was *"deally deally"*. My high school class had 10 boys and 15 girls. We had about 150 kids in the whole school that was from the 7th grade to 12th grade, so everyone knew everybody. We grew up at a wonderful time, just like the Happy Days TV show.

We had 2 hangouts. One was **Alotofwanna**. The Newtown bank is there now. The other was the **Highline** Restaurant. It is a dress shop now (Applause). We would race three abreast from Alotofwanna out the highway to Aquetong Road and then back again, driving oncoming cars off of the road. We didn't have any cops around then.

My Uncle Harry had a 1941 Chevy that he paid about $600 for brand new. Well one day he had an accident coming up to see us so he gave me his cracked up car with a bent frame. I found a good frame and decided to take the body off and change the frame. What a job but I did it. One day I just pulled my car into Mr. Schucks garage and started to work on it. I wanted to put dual exhaust on it. Being a 6 cylinder meant that I had to split the exhaust manifold and weld a new pipe into it. At first Mr Schuck started to cuss me out but then he would end up showing me how to do it. I had the only Chevy with real dual exhaust with Hollywood mufflers. Then I drilled holes about 6 inches from the end of the tailpipe and put spark plugs in them.

When you got up to about 60 mph, you would let up on the gas, pull the choke out and flip on the model T coil. This would make flames come out of the tailpipe about 3 to 4 feet long. Really cool stuff. At this time, I was working at Wes Hendricks gas station washing cars on weekends. We charged $175 to $200 if it had white walls.

There was a skating rink in Buckingham. It is Brown Brothers auction house now. It would close around 11:00 pm then everyone would race back to the Highline.

Well one night another friend, Dick Theile had a 1948 plymouth convertible that had a spotlight and a wolf whistle. We wrapped a red handkerchief around the spotlight and waited at Ingham Springs side of the road. Sure enough, Dick Towle and Leon Clark came speeding down the hill. We pulled out and chased them with the wolf whistle screaming and switching the spotlight behind them on and off. They thought we were the cops. We caught up with them around the Cartwheel (no longer there). Well Dick kept going but Leon pulled over thinking we were the cops.

One summer, my two best friends, George Davis (nicknamed, Tick) and Carl Otte (nicknamed, Ottie) wanted to go to the sea shore but we didn't have any money. Mel and Sarah would rent a house in Seaside Heights so we had a place to go. My Mom said she would give us $40 if we would paint our house. Well we didn't have a ladder so I shot an arrow with a string tied on it over the house. I then pulled a rope over and tied the rope around Ottie on one end with the other end to the bumper of my chevy. I pulled Ottie up the side of the house and we got it painted. We went to the shore and had a lot of fun.

Carl Otte

Working for Havie while bailing hay, we bailed 1200 bails and even stacked them into the barn. That was a real record. While fertilizing corn on Grover's, I lost my class ring somewhere in that field. I wonder if someone will ever find it. My wife doesn't believe that story but that's what really happened. She thinks I gave it to another girl or something.

In my junior year, our class was invited over to New York City by a junior class at Lincoln high School. Each member would take one of us home to stay overnight. This one boy took two of us, Ross Hendricks and myself. They lived in a big apartment with its own elevator. They had maids and a butler. At dinnertime, there was a big long table with the father at one end and the mother at the other, just like you see in the movies. I could not begin to tell you what we ate, but we both ate everything, bones and all. I remember the father asking us what time we would get up in the morning out on the farm. We felt really out of place. I was given their daughter's room to sleep in. It had its own bathroom and it had this funny looking box in the window that made a lot of noise. I never saw or knew what an air conditioner was. Their son had his own TV and a short wave radio (which I never even heard of) and a big train set all in his bedroom. They lived on Park Avenue and even had a doorman. His father's name was Ben and his last name was Lazarus or something like that. He took the first part of his first name and the last part of his last name and put them together which spelled BENRUS. He owned the big watch company. It was really quite a time.

Pictured: Ross Hendricks, Fred Glasby, Bruce Quinby, Jim Melson, Cynthia Smith, Claire Rufforce, Carl Otte

Solebury School was a big rival to our school. It was a private school for rich kids. It was a tradition to sneak up and take their school sign every year. It was always just a wooden pole and we would set it up at our school. One year, they put a new one using a 4 inch black pipe filled with cement. So Jimmy and I took hacksaws to saw it down only to break our saws. So then we got Blair Livezey. His Dad had a machine shop. Blair borrowed a big pipe cutter and we broke that. Then we got blankets to hold up while Johnie Paxson used a torch and we cut it down.

So Blair had his Dad's 1941 Chrysler 4 door sedan and John Scott had his Dad's 4 door sedan loaded with kids and we went to get the sign. Well, they were waiting for us with baseball bats. They came swinging their bats, trying to get the driver. Blair took off and the bat went through the back window. With that, Johnie pulled out to get away and hit the kid with the bat. We were going 100 mph down Solebury hill and didn't get caught. Later we found out the kid only had a broken collar bone. I think we stopped after that. We could have killed someone.

The headmaster at the school had a yellow jeepster convertible. Well, some of the guys borrowed Pat Poachers yellow jeepster and about midnight drove into the school by the dorms and fired off a couple of shotguns and then drove out the back entrance. They did this for 2 nights in a row. Then the headmaster came home late the next night and the kids were waiting for a yellow jeepster and they clobbered him, throwing chairs and stuff out the windows at him thinking it was our guys. Most of the time I just went along for the ride and though it was fun, now looking back on these events, I don't feel very proud of myself, but that's what kids did in those days. Little did I ever think that my brother in law, John Eichlin and my own son, Tony, would go to and graduate from Solebury School.

Some of these stories I am just writing down as I remember them and some may not be in order.

My hot rod had a 1 gallon tank mounted on the firewall filled with kerosene with a quarter inch line into the carborator. When you turned on the valve, it would put out a smoke screen you wouldn't believe. No one could fool you.

At the gas station, there was a guy who came around selling all kinds of stuff. One of the things I used to buy were these auto bombs. They had 2 long wires. You hooked one wire to a ground and the other to a spark plug. You let it hang down under the car. The rest of it was about 6 inches long. When they would start the car, there would be a really loud whistle and then a loud explosion with a lot of smoke. Really neat. One night, Dick Towle had his car parked in front of Dr. Libby's house (now the Mansion Inn across the street from Mayor Flood's house). Dick was dating Doc's daughter. I had the Mayor's son, Billy with me and we put one of these bombs on Dick's car, then we would wait until he came out and started the car, then drive past laughing. It ended up with the Mayor running down the street after us blowing his police whistle and Billy yelling "if he catches us I am dead". You had to know Billy Flood to appreciate this.

At school, a lot of times the kids would take a ride during lunch hour so naturally I would put a bomb on someone's car when it would go off the principal would come running out trying to find out who did it. It was a blast. Sometimes I even would put them on my own car.

Paul Whitman who was a big band leader, known as the father of jazz, started a rec center in Lambertville for kids to have a place to hang out with dances and events. One day they had a scavenger hunt. Some of the things you had to find was a hubcap off a 38 chevy. A lot of chevy's lost their hubcaps that night! Then you had to change a tire on your car. 2 guys to a car. You were timed on it. It was fun to see cars falling off of jacks and everything. Dick Shuck would always win.

One night, Jimmy Smoyer and I borrowed some blasting copper wire from the quarry and drove up to Frenchtown. There was a movie theater there it had a long parking lot. Everyone would park in a line. We would drape the copper wires down the line on their back bumpers and hook it up to my model T coil. When the show was over, everyone would get a pretty good shock when they touched their car. We heard all kinds of yells then we would take off!! It's a wonder we were never locked up only because we were never caught.

Going back a few years, I can remember our whole family including Grannie and Grand Pop and Aunt Ahmee all going to the 1939 World's Fair in New

York. It was really something. I think I have some old movies of it. Dad took us to a restaurant for dinner. You would watch people ice skate while you ate. The bill was over $100. That was really a big deal.

I guess times were hard during the depression because Aunt Ahmee and Uncle George moved in with us along with Harry and Evie Kelly, who moved into our basement. They were relatives and lifelong friends of our family.

PHILLIPS MILL

When Dad built our house on Phillips Mill Road, he had all cement floors with I beams. The stone was all handpicked for color. Back then if you had a radio, it had to have an aerial. So Dad put a special plug in every room, hooked up to hundreds of feet of copper wire strung in our attic. We had great reception. He also had a master switch in his bedroom that would turn on a light in every room in the house along with old car headlights mounted on the outside corners of the house. It really lit the place up. They didn't have outdoor spot lights back then in 1939 when the house was built. It also had a heater that would burn oil, wood or coal along with a generator for electricity. He was ready for anything.

My Dad had one younger brother, Rudy who was married to Josephine. They had Rhoda who was the same age as me and a younger brother, Rod, short for Rudy, and a sister Cynthia. (We were fortunate to have reconnected with them and enjoyed them so much).

My Dad was into everything. Besides a truck farm, we would grow 12 acres of watercress, chives, parsley, thyme, leeks, plus a lot of veggies. He had a 14 acre stone quarry, a sawmill and then started a produce business. I worked for him while growing up. My Dad seemed to be able to do anything that interested him from being an artist to welding.

Dad always had to have a big new car or the latest gadget. I loved my Dad and Mom very much and I just couldn't believe that he left us like he did. It was very hard being 14 and losing him like that. He went to Florida and married his first cousin. I saw him two times after that for a short visit. Later when I married, Judy and I lived in Florida but I never went to see him. It would have broken my mom's heart. He always smoked a pipe and always had a waxed mustache. I think he got throat cancer and took his own life a year before Mom died. I would like to think that my Mom and Dad would be proud of me and what I have become. I hope so. I just wish that

they could have known all of my kids. They would
have enjoyed them so.

High School Graduation 1953

About this time I started to date. My first girlfriend
ended up being a lesbian. So much for that. Then I
went with a girl in my class named Cynthia Smith for
a while but then I noticed a little red head named
Judy Eichlin and fell in love with her. She was 15 and
I was 17. I guess it was meant to be because 56
years later we are still married. Judy's dad, Bud, let

her go out with me so he could hunt and trap on our farm. Her mom wasn't too happy about it but she came around. In my senior year, 4 of us decided to quit school and join the Navy. Fred Glasby, George Davis, Denny Michner and myself went down to the recruiting office at Willow Grove Naval Base to sign up. The guy really reamed us out and said go back and finish high school and then we could sign up. So that is what we did. We signed up for 4 years. Judy wasn't happy about it but looking back it was a good choice. I left on the 15th of December for boot camp at Bainbridge Maryland. Never being away from home before, I was one homesick kid, especially on Christmas Eve. I can remember washing clothes, crying and singing Christmas songs, but I got over it. Havey took me down to Philly and when I was sworn in they made us mop and clean the office. In the middle of this they got a phone call from my Aunt Ahmee wanting to know if I could meet her for lunch at Wanamakers tea room. Well I could have just died. The first thing they did was split us up. When we got to boot camp we were given a 15 day leave. I never saw Fred again the whole 4 years. I saw Denny once in Jacksonville, Florida but George and I saw a lot of each other. Then they sent me to Norman Oklahoma for what they called A School. They gave you a week course on every job in the Navy and then tested you to see where you were best qualified. In my case, it was as an airplane mechanic.

Then they sent me by Pullman train to Memphis Tennessee to mechanic school. It was hard but they had good instructors and I made it. I then had a 15 day leave so I took a bus home. It took 40 hours before I left I went into town and bought a set of taylor made whites. I weighed 157 lbs soaking wet. I think that was the only time I wore them because I gained weight with all of the home cooking.

Then I was transferred to a squadron called HATU (pronounced hat 2). They had 2 beach crafts, 1 AD sky raider and 6 P2V's, 2 engine patrol bombers.

We trained navigators and bombardiers for dropping the A-bomb. It wasn't too long that I was put on a plane crew as a 3rd mechanic. Each crew had a plane captain, a 2nd mechanic and a 3rd mechanic. We had to take care of the plane, fuel it, clean it and one of us had to fly in it. We didn't have a seat. We knelt on our knees between the pilot and copilot. My job was to take care of all the engine settings, monitor all engine gauges, transfer fuel and oil. We had to know how much fuel we were using at all times and how much we had left.

We had to inspect the plane every hour and keep the piglets coffee cups full. We took turns flying, usually every 3rd bus trip. We got $75 a month extra for flying. I was fortunate enough to make 3rd and then 2nd class petty officer. Then they gave me my own plane all by myself which meant I had to fly every hop. After a while, they gave me a 2nd mechanic, Gail Smothers. That took the load off.

We would get a 30 day leave every year. Usually, I would take 2, 15 days at a time but being in Norfolk meant I could come home on weekends if I had a car. My sister had an accident with my old car so I bought a 1948 red chevy coupe. I thought I was hot stuff. The first weekend I stayed out late every night with Judy so when it was time to go, I was dead tired and had about an eight hour trip back to the base. I left at 8 pm on Sunday night. By the time I got on the Jersey turnpike, I was falling asleep. It was winter time and cold so I put all the windows down and the radio up loud to keep me awake. Somehow I made it to the end of the pike where I picked up 2 sailors hitch hiking and let them drive all the way back. I learned a good lesson that night. There was a Ferry you had to get and sometimes you had to wait 4 or 5 hours just to get on it. It was 21 miles long. Now it's a bridge tunnel system you drive over.

George Davis was stationed right across a river in Portsmith so we would go home together a lot. He had a 1949 Ford and I was driving home. There was a line of cars about six and we were all doing way over the speed limit. All of a sudden, Tick yelled and I locked up the brakes. We slid past the camaraderie. All of the cars in front of us got tickets

but they waved us through. That was the first time
we ever saw radar.

About this time, our outfit was moved to NAS
Sanford, Florida, a small town 12 miles north of
Orlando. Judy and I got engaged and then got
married. I was doing a lot of flying then. When we
took off we would fly right over our house. I had
over 430 hours logged in. One time we were flying
over the Bermuda triangle and we lost all of our
radios and compass but we were lucky it was a
sunny day. So we flew dead straight into the sun
until we hit the coastline.

One night, we were flying over the gulf of Mexico
when a very bright light came across the sky and
stopped right beside us for a few seconds and then
just flew away. All the radios went crazy reporting
this. The air force scrambled jets but they could not
find it. I guess it was a UFO. Who knows!!

Another time, I was so used to flying everyday that I
wouldn't bother to look where I was going. So we
took off, me wearing only a light flight suit. No hat,
no jacket and we went to SAC air force base in

Omaha Nebraska where it was about 4 below and snowing. I thought I would die. It was so cold especially coming from Florida with its 80 degree weather. Some guy felt sorry for me and lent me a jacket and gloves. We stayed overnight. We had a bunch of brass going to a meeting that we were trying to get the contract for the Navy to carry the A bombs. It was given to the Air Force. The next day it was really cold so I had two big heaters. One on each engine trying to get them warm enough to start. Someone behind me said, "Hey, how about putting one of those heaters inside the cabin?" Not looking to see who said it, I just replied, "bullshit, these engines don't start we can't get the hell out of here". Then I looked to see who it was. Naturally, it was a full captain so I added the word "Sir" and got away with it. The pilot was a lt. and the co- pilot was a full commander. As we were taxing the pilot noticed that we had no oil pressure on the number 2 engine and didn't want to continue. The commander asked me what I thought. I told him it was some condensation in the gauge and would be OK as soon as it warmed up. Adding the fact that I was going with them, the pilot even though being a junior grade really had command of the plane was mad as hell at me when the commander took my word for it and took over the command of the plane and off we went. Lucky I was right.

One day, my pilot came out to the plane. He was stone drunk and I didn't know if I should refuse to go or not so I asked another plane captain what to do. He said to put him on 100 percent oxygen so that's what I did and sure enough by the time we took off he was sober. You just didn't question any officer being an enlisted man.

We had one hot shot that when we were taking off he would always pull the wheels up before we were airborne so the plane would sort of settle and then pull up. They said it looked neat but was a little risky.

There was on old ship anchored in a lake and we would drop one 25 lb bomb at a time, training the bombardiers sometimes for 8 hours all day long. We always had to buzz the ship, making sure no one was on it. Well one time we saw 2 guys with a rowboat tied up to it. We opened the bomb bay doors and made a run on them. They were so scared one guy was rowing as fast as he could and the other guy had his feet over the back kicking like hell. It was really funny. We would take a razor blade, brake it in half and stick it into a coke bottle throwing it out of the plane. It would whistle like a bomb.

One time our skipper was throwing a party so he had us fly to Rhode Island for lobsters, Bermuda for booze, North Carolina for charcoal, Puerto Rico for rum and then the day of the party we flew all around picking up people to come to the party and afterwards taking them home. How is that for your tax dollars at work!

FLORIDA

When we lived in Sanford, Judy's grandmother, we called her Nana Grace and her sister, Aunt Helen, came down to see us on the train. Judy's Dad, Bud, gave Nana a box to bring down for my birthday. He told her it was a box of candy. When I opened it up, it was a P38 pistol. She had a fit when she realized she carried a gun on her lap all the way to Florida. We took them to Cypress Gardens which we all enjoyed very much. Not far from there was what they called Spook Hill. You drove your car down this hill, turned it off and put it in neutral. All of a sudden the car would start to roll backwards up the hill all by itself. We took them to a drive-in movie after they said they spend the whole time on their knees in order to see the movie. We loved them both very much and enjoyed having them stay with us. Another time, my brother Mel and Sarah came down to stay with us. Mel had all his money in a sock and kept it under the front seat. We took them down to Fort Lauderdale to see an old family friend of my Dad's. We had a hard time finding a motel that we could afford. We had fun with them. When they left, he took all of our oranges off our trees. Another time, friends of my Mom, Lin and Marion stopped to see us. It was great seeing all of these people from home.

We had our first Christmas together. It didn't seem right in 80 degree weather. We had a real tree and decorated it. The only thing we still have from those old decorations is a little paper angel for the top and it is still on our tree today. Dave and Sherri came over and shared the day with us.

Dave and I did a lot of hunting down there. He got into bow hunting. One day he shot a 40 lb bobcat. He had the whole thing mounted. I shot a 6 ft diamond back rattle snake. I hate snakes so I gave it to Dave. He made a belt out of it. It looked good. We had a lot of good times hunting together.

We had another good friend, Bill Redmond from North Carolina who hunted with us. We used to try to drop a coke bottle and draw our pistols and shoot it before it hit the ground. We all could do it with a little practice. But one day Willy shot himself in the knee. I think he still has that bullet in his knee! It was time to move on.

I still talk to Willy on the phone once in a while. Judy and I stopped to see him years later on one of our trips. He lives in Herndersonville, NC. Dave got discharged and went to work at Cape Canaveral at the space center. Everybody in our outfit had top secret clearance which made it easy to get a job there. Dave was from Hershey, PA but when he hit Florida he loved it and said he would never go back to PA, and he didn't.

All of a sudden, they broke up our outfit and we were transferred back to Norfolk.

I was transferred back to Norfolk, Virginia to an anti submarine squadron, VS 27. Being second class meant the Navy paid to move us. So off Judy and I went back to Norfolk. We only had enough money to stay in a motel one night so we had to find an apartment in one day which we were able to do. We found a nice place in Ocean View on the bay. It took all our money to pay all the deposits.

So there we sat with leave and couldn't come home. I called my Mom and she sent us $20 which was enough for us to drive home and back again. It was great seeing everyone. We stayed at Mom's.

In Norfolk, Judy got a job at a car dealer, Nick Wrights. She had to ride the bus to get there. My job was to be there at 6 a.m. every morning. I had 3 airplanes to take care of. They were a 2 engine plane with a crew of 3. So I didn't fly anymore. No more flute pay. I had to start each plane to check out the engines, pre flight them, fuel them and keep them clean. Once they took off I had nothing to do.

I was done work at 2 pm so I had a lot of time to fool around. Judy worked until 5 pm. We had to use a Laundromat to do our wash so the very first thing we bought was a washing machine on time. I had what they called 4 section duty which meant that every fourth day and every fourth weekend I had to stay on the base. That was hard for Judy. Sometimes if we had extra money I could pay someone to take my duty. We had a second floor apartment in an old beach house. It had a chimney in the middle of it so all the floors slanted away from the chimney. It was like walking around a mountain. If you spilled something you couldn't catch it. Ocean View had an amusement park and every Saturday night we could lay in bed and watch the fireworks. We bought a 14 ft boat with a 10 hp motor that I could play with. I had a lot of fun with it but every time Judy got into it, it would not run. It became quite a joke. One time I finally got it going so I was going to take Judy for a ride. Well before I knew it, we had a destroyer on one side of us and an aircraft carrier coming at us. I was scared to death. I was able to turn around and get the hell out of their way. Norfolk is the biggest Naval base in the world so there are always ships around. After that, I just stayed in our little bay.

The people that lived there had an Uncle Norman who was a real salt, had been all over the world. One day my boat just wouldn't hardly move. Uncle Norman said you better pull it out and scrape the barnacles off the bottom. Sure enough, it was loaded. It went like hell after that. I would try to pick Judy up from work whenever I could so she didn't have to ride the bus. When we left Florida we didn't see Dave and Sherry until years later. Our new friends were Leo and Jean Vallett. Leo was a mechanic in my outfit. They had a little boy who was real quiet. Leo would drink and gamble a lot, sometimes losing his whole paycheck in a card game and telling Jean that someone had stolen it. They had to buy a food plan in order to have food to eat. Leo never had any money. He stayed in for 20 years. We took our kids to visit them when Leo retired. They lived in Rhode Island. He had a lobster boat. We stayed overnight and ate our fill of lobsters. Years later they stopped to see us at the farm in a big RV camper. We lost contact with them after that.

One time I had to go on a 6 week cruise on the carrier, the USS Wasp. We had 2 destroyers and 25 planes to protect us and one submarine trying to sink us and planes would drop. Well, the first night out they sunk us four times. Made you feel good. It was very hot below deck and our bunks were 5 high with only about a foot and a half between them with very little ventilation. You kept all your stuff in your sea bag. They had about 50 men jammed into a small compartment. Working on the flight deck is one of the most dangerous jobs there was. All of these planes parked all close together, wings folded, engines running. One pilot walked into a prop and was killed. As soon as your plane took off, you got into the line shack so you were out of the way. I saw this guy looking at me from across the room. It turned out to be Bucky George Redfield who was a grade below me in school. Here we were in the same outfit and never knew it. The Wasp was a great ship. Good food, clean and high moral. Later, I was on another 6 week cruise on the USS Valley Forge, another aircraft carrier. We were sent to Cuba to evacuate any Americans. We had a squadron of helicopters.

Aunt Ahmee, Jerry Melson, Florence Blackwell, Barbara Melson, Sarah Melson and Anna Pass Melson

After arriving home, we stayed with my Mom and started looking for an apartment. I think I got about $1500 for mustering out of the Navy. We finally found one at Shady Lawn. It was a large home made into rentals located at Route 263 and Greenhill Road. It had a big bedroom, a big living room, a big kitchen and a small bedroom. My Mom was upset and said we didn't know what we were doing. She asked us if it had a refrigerator and we weren't sure. So we went back and asked the landlord. He said he had an old one in the basement that we could use. Judy's Mom and Dad gave us and old bed we could use. Mom gave us a table to eat on. Mel and Sarah let us borrow their lawn chairs to sit on so we had it made! Two boys had lived there before us and they asked the owner if they could paint the kitchen. Thinking this was a good deal, he said, "OK". Well, they painted the walls bright red, the ceiling black with red venetian blinds with black tapes. The owner had a fit and said he would re-paint it for us. Guess what? We loved it and kept it the way it was. Relatives started to give us furniture and before long we started to acquire things. Soon we had two sofas which was a good thing because we had to give Mel his lawn chairs back for the summer.

Judy was able to get a job at Ace Manufacturing Co. in Chalfont as a bookkeeper. We only had one car, my 1956 Ford that Judy used. I borrowed my Mom's pickup truck and started looking of a job. I had a hard time finding one but finally got one in Flemington at a furniture store (Bardens) delivering furniture. I had to use Mom's until I could find a car that we could afford.

Mel and Sarah had just bought their Mill in Solebury. It had 3 houses on it. Judy became pregnant with our first child so we moved into a small apartment in the top floor of one of their houses. I got two more jobs part time. One was at Wes's gas station on Wednesday nights. The other was at Bob Heath's,

(Dad's) station on weekends. I worked from 6 pm until 1 am on Saturday and Sunday nights. We also had a puppy that Bud gave us. He was a springer spaniel named Tiger that we loved very much.

I finally found a 1953 Ford convertible with its motor all apart in a box for $65. I put it all back together and it ran OK. Judy became friends with a girl at work whose husband worked at Paul Histands in Cross Keys and said they were looking for a mechanics helper. At lunchtime I called and got to talk to Mr. Histand himself. Well he hired me over the phone without even meeting me. I started at $1.25 an hour. Judy bought me new work clothes so I would look nice. Nobody told the foreman that I was coming to work so he was mad when I showed up. He put me on the steam cleaner for 3 days. It just ruined my new clothes, giving me a lot of burns. Then he put me in the farm shop and told me to put together a machine which I never saw before. One of the other mechanics told me I had it upside down and told me how to do it and I made out OK. Then I was moved to the truck shop. I learned a lot working there and stayed there for 9 years. When I left I was making $1.95 an hour, clearing and bringing home about $43 a week.

POINT PLEASANT PIKE

By this time we had a baby girl named Pamela Ann born December 6, 1959. We were so happy but very crowded. My Mom sold the farm to the quarry and moved to my sisters. We started looking for a house to buy and found a nice 3 bedroom ranch house on Point Pleasant Pike with 2 acres. I think it cost about $23000. My Mom gave us $10000 to put down on it. So now we had a nice big house to live in. It even had a 2 car garage that was heated and I could take in jobs for extra money. We moved in using pickup trucks. It seemed so big. Judy and I would get lost in it until we got used to it. It raised a lot of eyebrows at work, buying such an expensive house. It had a big lawn and took forever to mow with the small mower that we had. Judy would try to do it during nap time but it was a job. So again I bought a riding mower in a box all apart for $35, got it running and it made a big difference. Harry Getz tried it out and ran over one of Judy's rose bushes.

February 7, 1962, our son, Jim Jr. was born. Again, we were thrilled. There was a tradition at work that you had to treat everyone to ice cream when you had a baby or it was your birthday. Jimmy and I both being in February took all of our extra meal money for the whole month, but it was worth it.

I left Histands to work for more money at Bucks Products, a cement company, taking care of their trucks. It didn't work out so I went back to Histands.

They were mostly Mennonites that worked there. At Christmas time they gave you 5 silver dollars plus one for every year you were there and a meal at the Cross Keys Diner.

Judy got really mad at me because I wouldn't take a vacation. Little did she know that I took the money instead. I also saved up my money from weekend jobs. I bought her a Singer sewing machine with some lessons as a surprise. Well she went wild making clothes for everybody. She made coats, even made her sister's wedding dress. Then she started to learn to quilt. Over the years, I think she has made at least 30 or 40 quilts, everyone just beautiful. She is still at it today. She has a group of friends that meet once a week. She can't sit still without working on something. She also joined the Jr. Women's Club in Doylestown. One time she was on a safety committee and went to Harrisburg for a meeting. Our daughter Jane was born then and only about 2 weeks old. So I stayed home to take care of the kids. By 10:00 am I had about 40 diapers washed and on the clothes line. I had Jane in a baby coach, Jimmy and Pam playing in their sand box while I had a tractor trailer in our driveway all apart putting new brakes on it. A UPS guy stopped by with a package and couldn't believe what he saw. Jane was born on April 6, 1965.

We would buy a load of dirt and dump it in the driveway. The kids, mostly Jimmy, would play in it for hours. Once I bought a Model A frame and chassis. It only had a steering wheel and a transmission and wheels. Jimmy couldn't stay away from it. I think he must have put a million miles on it, just sitting in our driveway. Years later, he sold it and made some money on it.

THE STATION

Again, I left Histands and went to work for Sylvan pools on the night shift. I think I worked from 6 pm to 2 am. That was hard to get used to but the money was good. It wasn't long until they made me night foreman. One night I was in 5 different states, fixing trucks that were broken down. Paul Gares who worked at Histands always said that we should go in business together. Every time I found a garage for sale, he would chicken out. My Mom died and left us some money. We went a little wild and bought a new car for $2,000 and had a 20 ft. by 40 ft. swimming pool put in for $2,000. Also enough to start our own garage. A Shell station became available in New Hope at Sugan Road and Rt. 179 so we jumped on it. I took it over from Rip Johnson and it even came with a 1950 Ford pickup that we called Blue Bird. Gas sold for 32.9 cents a gallon. I was scared to death but with Judy in back of me, how could I lose. There were a ton of funny stories. I wish I could remember them all. Every Sunday morning I had to find the police car. I never knew who was on duty the night before, so I had to drive around to find it. Once I found it, I would leave Blue Bird there and had to bring it in, service and wash it. I worked by myself so I had to do this before I opened. One day when I got to the station, I found it broken into so I called the police. It was really funny to see them flying down the road in Blue Bird. Unfortunately they couldn't catch a fly if they tried. One day they stopped a car and left the police car sitting on the train tracks. You guessed it, the train ran over the police car.

I finally hired a guy to help out in the daytime and some kids to work nights and weekends. I was able to get an inspection station and that made a big help. Back then, you had to get your car inspected 2 times a year. Once on the last day, I had 50 cars on the lot waiting to be done. We also would wash and wax a car for $25. I had to write a check for the first load of gas for over $2000. I was really shook. I had to keep the books everyday and didn't bother to count the pennies. Judy had a fit so I had to count all of the pennies. Finally Judy took over the bookkeeping.

One day a man came in and gave me a $100 bill and said to let him know when he used it all and he would give me another one. His name was Bob Hightower. He was a little bit of a nut but became a good customer. Besides, I had never seen a $100 bill before.

Back at the gas station, things were going pretty good although I usually ended up working a lot of hours. I had to pay Shell Oil Company a cent and a half on every gallon of gas that I sold. The more you sold, the more rent you paid.

There were only 2 gas stations in New Hope. Paul Nash had the other one just up the street. Well, he put it up for sale and we bought it for $70,000. Our mortgage payment was $424 per month and I wondered how on earth I could ever pay that much.

We settled on July 1st 1970. So now we had 2 gas stations. Paul's was a Sinclair that just changed to BP when I took over. Shell wanted to move with me so we negated a deal that they would renovate the building plus add on a 3rd bay. This seemed like a good deal. I finally gave up the old station. They knocked it down and built a Mobil station. When I bought the new one a man named Howard Higgins came with it and worked for me until he retired. I think every kid in New Hope worked for me at one time or another. They usually caused more problems than they were worth. I always said I could write a book on just my employees and then another book on customers. There were so many good and funny stories. As soon as the kids were old enough they would help out and work for me. Judy said I made workaholics out of them. Forty years later, four of them are running the place.

We were doing pretty good. Had the pool and had a lot of pool parties. The kids really loved it. Every special day, Judy would buy a thousand bricks and a load of sand for me to make a patio around the pool By the time I got done, we had a 12,000 brick patio and it looked great if I do say so myself.

Our house had a porch facing the pool so I hired Lester Stockton to close it in with big windows. He was a cop for New Hope and did this on the side. We loved it so much we moved the dining table, TV and our chairs out there and literally lived out there all of the time. It was even heated. Later on we even had a pool heater put in so we could use the pool longer. I used to enjoy taking care of the pool and the house. It was a neat house, 3 bedrooms, big living room, dining room combination. It had radiant heat in the floors, even in the garage. It had a little barn and we bought a pony named Katie for Pam and the kids to ride on. She must have been an old circus pony or something. All you had to do was walk in front of her and she would follow you forever. She would always run up to the fence to greet me when I came home from work. By this time Tommy was born, July 13, 1969.

PINE RUN FARM

I remember going up to Pickerings in Gardenvile and buying our first color TV for our bedroom so we could watch the moon landing. It wasn't very big but it was great. We were great. The station was doing great. We had the world by the ass!

Next thing you know Judy was pregnant again with Tony and we started looking for a bigger house. We looked at quite a few homes all over the place. One day Judy found this old farm house just outside of Doylestown and we made an appointment to see it.

Before I go any further, I should tell you that if Judy even sees a mouse, she gets hysterical and I mean hysterical. When we pulled into the parking lot it was raining. When we opened the door to get out of the car, there was a dead RAT. I thought that would do it, but I was wrong. Judy kept going. The man that answered the door was wearing a bathrobe and not much else, but Judy kept going. What we called the gun room was very dark and dirty. It had doors on the walk-in fireplace and when I opened them to look inside it was half full of trash and beer cans. Judy kept going. The kitchen, actually the whole house was filthy. But the hot water faucet would not turn off so it steamed all the time. We couldn't see three rooms off of the kitchen. It was an apartment. We were told that it had 2 rooms and a bath. The dining room wasn't too bad but entering the living room there was dog shit all over. Judy kept going. Upstairs there were 4 bedrooms and 2 baths of which we saw 3 of the bedrooms and one bath. The owner was locked in one bathroom and a man was locked in another. We came downstairs and I asked Judy if I should look in the basement? She said she wouldn't go down there in a million years. So, off I went. It was pretty bad with about 4 inches of water all over. When I opened the door to the barn all you saw were RATS running all over. There were 40 cows in the barn which was rented to a farmer down the road. Judy kept going! She looked at the realtor and said we would take it. The realtor nearly fell over. They were asking $125,000 and we offered $65,000 and they took it.

Now we had to sell our house and we did to a couple from New York City. Their teenage daughter was getting into trouble with drugs and the wrong crowd so they wanted to get her out of that environment. We went to the darn settlement for Pine Run and they announced that they weren't going to move out for another two weeks but they needed our money to buy another house. Judy told our lawyer to figure out how much rent to charge them. We finally got them out and got the farmer's cows out. Now we had one hell of a job before us. I took Mel through it and showed him everything. He said we were crazy and went home to take a shower.

One of my customers, Don Russ, was jack of all trades and he owed me a lot of money so I got him to help get the house livable. He did an outstanding job. We could not have done it without him. The windows were even spray painted on the outside with overspray. You could hardly see out of them. After a new kitchen, bathrooms, floors sanded and stained, the whole place scrubbed and painted, we were ready to move in. Don worked the days and I worked every night after work. There were times that I even got scared in that big empty house late at night working away by myself. Judy being pregnant couldn't really do too much although she still did a lot. I went to the store and bought a box of rat poison for the barn. I checked it the next day and the whole box was gone. Back to the store I went and I got a whole case. This really cleaned them out. We didn't even see a mouse for the next 25 years. Judy had a vision of this place and she was right.

Selling our house in Gardenville didn't go as easy as we thought. The night before settlement, their teenage daughter committed suicide by jumping off of their 10th floor apartment. I guess she couldn't handle moving. You can imagine how her mom and dad felt. We were sure that they would back out of buying our house, but they didn't. They asked for a 2 week extension. We wouldn't have blamed them if they had. They were just devastated. Anyhow, they still wanted to buy the place. They had a gift shop in New Hope. You couldn't even imagine how devastated they must have felt.

A few weeks after they moved in they asked me to stop by to explain some things about the pool and things. When I entered the house, I saw life size picture cutouts of their daughter standing in every room. I felt so bad for them. I don't think the mother was ever the same again. How could you ever deal with something like that.

Meanwhile, back at Pine Run, after the house was clean, we then tackled the barn, junk cars in the backyard, a lot of shingles missing on the roof, boards missing on the sides. We jack hammered the whole floor out of the downstairs barn, poured new floors, and had the roof fixed. Judy hand scraped all the white wash off all the beams and painted them.

Once we had a sit down dinner for 25 people in the barn. After I got the upper floor cleaned out I started to store cars and boats. This would pay for the upkeep of the barn. I could get 12 to 15 boats or cars on the top floor. One year we had a good snow plow year so we had the barn painted. Rick Knoster sprayed it. The barn took 90 gallons of paint. For the next 26 years we had many, many good times at Pine Run Farm. Girls scouts, Boy scouts, football, soccer games...Judy and I did it all. But all of a sudden our kids were all grown up, married and moved away. It took a lot of work to keep even just the lawn mowed. I even had a 50 ft. shooting range in the lower part of the barn. I also made a work shop and a heater for it. We bought a bar with mirrors and everything from what used to be The Young Man's Republic Club and it looked good. We also had a pool table. We had many hours of enjoyment in our barn. I guess that is about when I had my heart attack and we decided to look for a smaller house. We put the farm up for sale. I think it took about a year to sell it. We bought the farm in 1973 and stayed there for 26 years. I think we got somewhere around $460,000 for it. Tony was also born in 1973.

ONE OF MANY MEMORABLE STORIES

Judy went on another trip with the women's club and we were going to meet her at the Allentown airport around 5 o'clock with all the kids and then take them out to dinner. Tony was 6 months old and in diapers. I always tried to keep a $50 dollar bill in my wallet for an emergency but for a surprise for Judy, I used it to buy a dishwasher and had it installed.

We had a 69 buick station wagon and on the way up, we were about one mile from the airport when it broke down. A man stopped to help us but I told him that I could probably fix it but I couldn't. This was also during the gas shortage so most of the gas stations were closed. Luckily the same man that stopped before stopped back and offered to help. I asked him to give us a ride to the airport so we could meet Judy and he did. I think her plane was about an hour late, the kids were going wild. Tony had a wet diaper and I didn't bring any with me. When she finally got there I told her to watch the kids while I walked back to work on the car. Well I could not fix it so I walked back. We tried to rent a car but we didn't have any credit cards back then and we didn't have enough money between us because I spent my 50 bucks. Well I called Mel to see if he could come and get us. They were just sitting down to a dinner party and asked if I could get someone else. Then we tried to get a cab but because there were seven of us it would have to take two cabs. As a last resort we called Judy's mom and dad and they came to get us. But they came in their VW beetle instead of their bigger car. Bud turned the motor off but left the headlights on. We got everyone and the suitcases jammed into the VW. When Bud tried to start the car the battery was dead. I got out and pushed the car and finally got it started. By this time everyone was hungry. The kids were tired and crying. Tony was dripping wet, but we were on our way home. We got home about midnight. Judy didn't even notice the new dishwasher. That really made my day. The next day I got Pete Heath to tow our car back. It had a broken distributor shaft. What a night we had.

Sarah's sister had a beach house in Ocean City, MD and we started to rent it for a week for our vacation. We really loved it. We always took Nana Grace with us. She always wanted to bake a birthday cake for Judy. We always went on her birthday. Well, by the time it was over, Judy had made the cake. One year Donna and Sam came with us. We shared the cost.

One time Judy and I left Nana home to watch the kids while we took a sail boat ride for about 2 hours. When we got back she was all upset and crying thought we were never coming back and we had drowned. So much for leaving her alone.

Once we were coming home and blew a radiator hose. I was able to pull into a fast food place so they could go in and enjoy the air conditioning. It had to be in the high 90's while I worked on the car. Believe it or not I had a spare hose and tools with me. So I pulled the car around back and even found a shade tree to work under and had it fixed in about a half hour. Nana was again crying and thought that she would never get home again. She didn't realize how lucky we were. We loved Nana very much and wouldn't think of going to the shore without her.

I think we paid about $400 for a week but then she sold it and the new owners wanted $800 a week with a 2 week minimum. That put us out of the picture so we started looking for a new place to rent.

We couldn't find one that we could afford and ended up buying a house in Bay View Park, but now I am getting ahead of myself.

DELAWARE HOUSE

Looking for a house to rent for our yearly vacation, we started driving home, stopping at every realtor's office that we could find. Either they were all booked up or too expensive. Stopping at a realtor in South Bethany finding they didn't have any rentals. I said if you don't have anything to rent what do you have for Sale? Well this started something. They took us into Bay View Park and showed us a brand new house on a canal. They said that it would not last long on the market. I think it was around 64,000. We said we would think it over and continued looking all the way up the Jersey coast not finding anything available.

When we got home we asked if Bud and Marion would go in with us on buying a shore house. They declined. I think they thought we would end up fighting over who got to use it. When we called the realtor back to make another appointment to look at it again, she said that it was sold already. But there was another home that just came on the market on the same street furnished and that the owners would take the mortgage. So back we went to look at this house. We liked it and decided to go for it.

When we were signing the papers another person called to buy the place. This meant that we would have 3 mortgages going at the same time. We went to the New Hope Solebury bank , told them I wanted to remodel our kitchen at the farm for about $10,000 which we instead used for part of the down payment.

By this time I had a nice gun collection and would sell some of the better ones to help with the down payment which I did and we got the house. We had to rent it out for a few years to make all the payments. We finally got to the point that we could keep it for ourselves. We even bought a little boat, a runabout and started enjoying our new beach house for ourselves.

I still wonder how Judy came up with all the money to keep everything afloat. I know it wasn't easy but she did it and I admired her for it. I would have blown the whole thing. We give a week to all our kids plus Judy's brother John and his family and her sister, Kathy and her family. It's also available to anyone whenever it's not being used. We enjoy it in the winter time as much as the summer. We try to go down at least once a month. It's just an

enjoyable place. Beautiful beaches, great restaurants, plus a lot of things to do. At this time I think we have had it for 38 years. I hope that it will stay in the family for everyone in the future to enjoy. This year, 2012, was the first time that it flooded but only 2 feet in the garage. The water came within 2 inches from getting into the house. We were lucky. A lot of people got flooded pretty bad all because of Hurricane Sandy.

DOYLESTOWN HUNT

When we sold the farm, we bought a home in Doylestown. 230 Tether Way where we lived for 11 years. It was in Doylestown Hunt. It was a 3 bedroom house. We called it our plastic house compared to our stone farm house with 18 inch walls, but it suited us very well. It had a great family room that we lived in most of the time. I had a great workshop in the basement. I even made a 12 foot totem pole in the back yard.

It had a big drainage ditch in the back yard so I built a 16 foot bridge over it. You could even ride a lawn tractor over it.

With both of us with failing health problems, Judy couldn't even drive at night anymore, we resided to sell our house and move back to New Hope. Her brother inherited her Dad's house and said it could be used by anyone in the family that needed it. This was right behind our station and with walking distance to the shopping center and bank. This made it very convenient. We hired an architect to draw up plans for an apartment over the garage plus doing a master bedroom and redoing the porch by closing it in with glass. We still haven't heard a word from him.

THE GLASS HOUSE

Meanwhile Johnny bought another house about 2 blocks away with a 30 by 60 foot pool. It is very modern with a lot of glass. We call it the glass house. The 2 windows in the living room are 7 feet wide and 11 feet tall with a big sunken in fireplace. It's just a fun house, so John offered it to us to live in. One problem is, it would flood once in a while. John worked his butt off getting it ready for us. He redid the whole patio and had Tim, Jane's husband, build a wall around the house to keep the water out. It had 2 sheds and we started to move a lot of stuff in. John repainted the whole inside and it looked great.

They were calling for a hurricane and John asked us to stay overnight to keep an eye on everything. I took a pump and a wet vacuum along with 2 pumps that John had, I figured we were ready. We built a barricade in front of the opening in the wall. We also took Jane's triplet girls with us. Well the rain started. I had all the pumps ready. About 10 pm I was tired and went to bed. Judy and the girls stayed up. About midnight she woke me up and said the water was coming in so I started all the pumps. The next thing I knew the water was coming over the barricade and filling up the pit. Jane called and wanted her girls out of there. Jane and Tim tried to come in the driveway and couldn't make it. She called the fire company to rescue us. They tried for an hour to get into us. They even tried to get Stockton's air boat but they wouldn't come. Finally the firemen came down over the hill from Old York Road with ropes tied on trees and took the girls, one at a time on their shoulders. Then Judy and our dog, Mattie. We went thru water almost up to our armpits. We lost our car and a lot of trees. What had caused the flood was the railroad bed acted like a dam until it finally gave way, sending about 4 feet of water at us. Then the same week, another storm hit and the water came over the wall putting 18 inches in the whole house. I had a lot of my wood and tools in the pool shed and the whole shed was gone. John and Tim re did everything on the first floor. All new kitchen cabinets, dry wall, hardwood floors, new carpeting and re painted. The place looked beautiful. Judy and I went to our shore house just to get away. We finally sold our house in Doylestown and needed a rest. When we came back our kids had completely moved us into the glass house. What a load they took off of us.

Now we are living there. When they said another storm was on its way, we just got a Uhaul truck and moved out the first floor just in case. The storm Sandy, wasn't bad at all so we moved back in. We had to get another car. Our new address is 308 West Mechanic St, New Hope, PA. Yesterday John bought a horn of a Narwhal. It's a whale in Alaska. It's 8 feet long. Now we have to find a place for it. His friend Eric gave us a set of moose horns. We put them on the shed. Judy is just thrilled with all this stuff.

VACATION TRIPS

We had a lot of neat trips, the first of course was with Kathy to Bermuda which was great.

I think it was around 1968 when Judy's sister, Kathy, graduated from high school. She went to Villa Joseph Marie in Holland. For their class trip they took a cruise to Bermuda and needed some chaperones to go along. Having never been on a cruise before, Judy and I went along. I think it was around $400 bucks. We sailed out of New York City right past the statue of Liberty. When we got to our cabin, all of our luggage was already there but our cabin door was wide open and we didn't have a key to lock it. We didn't want to leave all our stuff and we didn't want to miss the Bon voyage party going on up on deck. Finally I found someone to ask. They assured us that it was OK to leave and that there was a cabin steward that would guard our cabin. So off we went. That part was great and what a beautiful site it was as we left the city.

By this time it was time for dinner so we went directly to dinner. We never dreamed it would be so great. When we returned to our cabin all our things were unpacked and put away. The beds were turned down and our night clothes were laid out on the bed. Well I couldn't stand this so every night before dinner I would hide my pajamas and every time we came back they would be there on the bed. Once I even stuffed them into the nozzle of the fire hose. Sure enough there they were on the bed when we came back. We would always find our cabin door wide open along with all the cabin doors. I never got to see this guy and couldn't figure out where he hid. On the last night I was going to wear them under my clothes to dinner but Judy wouldn't let me. She said I was nuts. Anyhow it was a wonderful trip. We took Kathy and a couple of her friends to a night club and saw a group called The Teachers. We also had a blast touring the island. We hired a cab for the day and he took us everywhere. That was the best way to see everything. Judy's two grandmothers watched the kids for us.

The strangest thing was that Judy was pregnant with Tom at the time and had morning sickness pretty bad. She wasn't sure if she could even go, but as soon as the ship started to rock and roll, she felt fine. No more morning sickness which was great.

Bermuda is a beautiful place and everyone should try to go there at least once in their lifetime. When I was in the Navy we flew there all the time for booze. It was really cheap. One other time we flew there on a trip with National Auto Parts and stayed at the Sonesta Inn. Judy broke a tooth and we had to find a dentist which we did and even got him to come in on a Sunday to fix it for her. We were lucky!

National Auto Parts who I bought most of our parts from used to take us on trips once in a while. We flew back to Bermuda on one trip. We also flew to Italy and had a wonderful time. It was paid for by Motorcraft. That was the parts department of Ford. We even stayed a couple of extra days. They had a toga party. Everyone wore togas. We were sitting at a table when the door flew open and in came two white horses pulling a chariot with the head man in it from Ford. It was really something to see. Then six Roman soldiers would carry in all the food in big pots and place it on a real fire right in the dining room. It was unreal.

National took us on a bus trip to a resort in Virginia Beach. The first thing that happened was the air conditioner on the bus stopped working and it was very hot. When we arrived at the resort it was raining cats and dogs and all the bell hops disappeared so we had to carry our own suitcases in the pouring rain. At dinner there were no prices on the menus so most of the guys ordered chicken. Judy and I ordered the most expensive. Come to find out all the dinners were the same price. The guys stole everything that wasn't bolted down, but we had fun.

We used to go on a lot of trips with our friends, Janice and Carl Slack, Marlene and Leon Clark and of course, Judy and I. All the girls went to first grade together and stayed good friends. I may not have these trips in order but I am doing the best I can. We all flew out to Vancouver and took the train ride back through the Rocky Mountains. There was a limo waiting for us at the airport. We would stop every night and stay in hotels for dinner and entertainment. Then continue on our trip the next day. We went up on glaciers. Before we left Vancouver we went to Stanley Park. That was neat. One of the places we stayed at was Lake Louise in Canada. That night we went to dinner and it was fabulous. They gave me the bill and for the six of us it was $1500. For breakfast in the morning it was $700. Fortunately it was all included in our trip. We still have a good laugh about it. All in all, it was a wonderful trip.

We went on a cruise to the Panama Canal. While at sea we got an SOS from a ship in trouble and we picked up 4 men in a life raft who had left their ship. Later we found their ship floundering with no power. There were still men on the ship but they didn't have any food or water. We shot a line over to them and gave them supplies. They asked our captain to call for a tow boat which he did and we continued on. It was quite exciting.

We stopped at Aruba and at San Blas Island which was about two feet above sea level. One good wave would have wiped them out. The canal was interesting. It cost $100,000 for the ship to go through it. We stayed in Costa Rica which was very nice and visited Nicaragua then flew home. That was where I first had a problem with my eye sight.

Judy and I took a trip by car to Nova Scotia. We stayed at Peggy's Cove at a B&B. We visited the graves of the Titanic disaster in Halifax. It was very moving and sad. We also stayed at some really neat places. Then we took a ferry to Prince Edward

Island. It was beautiful. We came back over the
New Federation Bridge, about 20 miles long over the
ocean to Canada. We stayed and saw the reversing
falls. They have a 20 to 30 foot tide change and
these falls really change direction.

One year we bought a new custom GMC van and off
we went. We took Judy's folks and Tony with us.
We went to North Dakota to see Mt. Rushmore. We
saw the wind caves, went into gold mines, saw a lot
of buffalo, went to see Crazy Horse. His arm was
stretched out pointing to something. They said a
hundred men could stand on his arm. That was how
big it was. The whole thing was carved out of a
mountain just like Mt. Rushmore. We went to a
burial site where there were a lot of mastodon
bones, one on top of another. They also discovered
the skeleton of a short nosed bear, really rare. I
expected to see John Wayne coming over a hill at
any moment. We saw the bad lands, Wild Bill's
home, the mile high saloon. We had a ball. Every
time we stayed at a motel, Bud would take all the ice
that they had to keep his beer cold. He also would
take all the pamphlets they had. He was a real joy.

One great bus trip with the gang was to Mackinac Island and we stayed at the Grand Hotel. Too beautiful for words. They didn't allow any motor vehicles, just horses on the island. The front porch of the hotel was longer than a football field. The food was out of this world. We took a ride on the Great Bear Sand Dunes. It constantly moves. We went to the Ford museum on the way home.

One of the best trips that I enjoyed was a cruise to Alaska. It was a Princess trip and they couldn't do enough for you. We flew to Vancouver where we got our ship and returned by land. We did it all. Helicopter ride to a glacier, plane ride around Mt. McKinley, train ride to Dinali. We flew out to Kodiak Island to see the big Kodiak brown bears. We even went up the Arctic circle. Great trip!! Just Judy and I went.

We took another cruise with the gang to the Mediterranean. It started in Amsterdam and I think it ended up in Rome. We hit the Chanel Islands, France, Spain, Portugal, Monte Carlo, Spanish Morocco and Italy.

One time we took a bus trip for Valentine's weekend to the Von Trapp resort. The trip was a disaster. The resort was nice but our bus driver ruined it for us by turning off the engine overnight. It was like 40 below and he could not restart it. Everyone froze all the way back through the snowstorm. I guess you can't win them all.

At the gas station, the oil companies used to have promotions and one was we gave a hot wheels toy car with a fill up. At the time we didn't have any grandchildren so one day I put a box full of hot wheels up in the attic to save until we had some grand kids. I think it was in the late 60's. Years later, I got them down and we realized that they were worth some bucks. Jimmy and Ellen put four of them on Ebay for about $1000 and when she hit the enter button, the phone started ringing. She sold them right away. To make a long story short, we ended up with about $7000 which we started a Disney fund.

For our 50th anniversary, we took our whole family to Disney. I can't begin to tell you what a wonderful time we had. I hope that someday we can do it again, although Tom got sick but he made it.

Another time, Judy and I drove to North Carolina and went to the Biltmore. It was really something to see. We visited an old Navy buddy and then went to Texas to see my brother who had just built a house on a big lake. We stayed with them for a few days and then drove up to St Louis to stay with another Navy buddy and his wife. Gail and Mary Lou Smothers. They took us all over. We went up the Arch and then to Branson which was great. On the way home we stayed at John and Beth's house in Clarion and then home.

Trip to California with Marion and Bud

Sunoco had a dealer meeting in San Francisco and we took Judy's folks with us. Bud was a riot. He couldn't believe that all the food and drinks were free. He had a ball. From there, we rented a car and drove to Yosemite to see the giant trees. We had dinner at the famous lodge. Bud complained that there was no TV. From there we drove down through Big Sur. What a ride that was. We also saw an event on the Queen Mary. What a ship. Bud came home from Europe when WWII was over on the Queen Mary. We saw the Spruce Goose. I think it was the biggest plane ever built. We went to see the Hurst Castle. It was unbelievable. We went to Palm Springs for a few days and to Long Beach for a plane home.

Another time we and the gang flew to San Diego and boarded a ship for a cruise to Hawaii. One of the stops we had to use tenders (life boats) to go from the ship to the dock. We had a trick rain storm and had to return to the ship. Our driver was just learning to drive the boat. First he almost backed into another boat. When we finally got turned around, a big wave hit us knocking out the front windows and swamping the whole boat. Everyone was soaked to the skin. When we finally reached the ship it was very rough. You had to jump from the life boat to a steel ramp on the side of the ship. One lady missed and got her leg caught between the boat and the ramp ending up in a wheel chair. It was beautiful there and we really enjoyed ourselves but I don't think that I would want to live there. When we left we sailed past a live volcano. At night you could see the red hot lava coming down the side of the mountain. At one point the water was 17 mile deep under the ship. When I am in water I like to be able to touch bottom with my feet!! We stopped in Mexico for a few hours and then back to San Diego then home. These were a few of our big vacations. We also had a lot of small trips with a lot of good memories.

PAM

Pamela Ann was our first child. Born December 6, 1959. We lived in a small 2 room apartment on the 2nd floor of my brother's house on Cuttalossa. You had to crawl over the bed to get to the crib. The bathroom was downstairs. It was pretty cramped.

When we moved to Gardenville, she had her own bedroom. She spent the next 11 years growing up there. Nursery school, kindergarten, grade school, all kinds of lessons, guitar, dancing, and swimming. We bought her a pony named Katie. When she was small we had a set of flash cards. I would show her just a tiny bit of it and she would name it. She had them all memorized.

One time she got into trouble. She sort of decorated our neighbor's house with crayons. He was not a happy camper. When we moved to the farm she had a ball playing detective. She finger printed everyone and kept a file of everyone. She swore that someone was murdered down in the woods behind our house. She built a tree house in the woods. When she was old enough, I took her hunting for small game and later on, deer hunting. I took her on a private hunt at a private club and she shot a white pheasant.

She played her guitar at church, she even wrote a couple of songs. For high school, we sent her to a private girls school, Villa Joseph Marie in Holland where she excelled at everything she did. I taught her how to drive. It was a little scary, but we made it. When she was old enough, she started working at our station, pumping gas, cleaning windshields and restrooms. For college she went to Mansfield and graduated with a degree in criminology.

She married John Mucha and lived in Scranton. It didn't last long and they got a divorce. She married again to Bill Abele and had a still born baby boy. Judy and I both held him in our arms. He was just beautiful. Makes you wonder why God took him so young. They named him William after his dad. He is buried at Thompson Memorial in our lot.

Then they had a beautiful baby girl they named Jennifer who is turning out to be a beautiful young girl. Then came Melanie, also a beautiful baby. She looks like her dad where Jen looks like her mom. Judy and I are so proud of them both. Pam and Bill are now separated and I feel so bad for them both. I know what it's like not having a dad around.

JIM JR.

James Pass Melson Jr, our second child and first boy was born on February 7, 1962. Jimmy, from the day he was born, loved cars and trucks. He would line them up the whole length of our living room. Growing up, he went to Mt. Carmel, he also loved to draw pictures. With his middle name PASS, which is on the Liberty Bell, we started him collecting anything with a Liberty Bell on it. Today you name it and he has it. Ice and roller skating, Cub Scouts and Boy Scouts, he did it all. He even made Eagle Scout. He went to LaSalle High School and then to LaSalle College for a year. College not being his thing, he came to work with me at the station. He married Ellen and they have 12 acres in Carversville. He is a good hunter and an outdoors man. He now has 2 antique cars which he loves. He is our head mechanic and the President of Melson's Service Center. Jimmy, like all of our kids, would do anything for you.

JANE

April 6, 1965 our Jane was born. Another beautiful baby girl. How lucky could we get! Judy used to say that Jane was the perfect baby. She even potty trained herself. Again, with all the lessons from ice skating to horseback riding, she always excelled in anything she did. She blew through grade school at Mt. Carmel where all of our kids went and then she went to Wood High School.

She loved horses, so naturally we had to buy her a horse. We put up a fence, which it got out of right away. I built a stable in our barnyard. Every morning she would take it out to the field and would carry out water for it plus clean out the stable. We had Ty until she went to college at Del Val where she wanted to live in the dorm. This meant the horse had to go. I still can't believe we were able to sell the horse so easily but we did. Jane, along with her sister, is a First Class Girl Scout. I remember teaching her how to drive which she did easily. I bought her an old Ford maverick and fixed it up for her first car. After college she got a job with Jamesway where she went up the ladder to manager training.

She married Gary Gatto and was lucky enough to
have triplet girls, Cary , Grace and Samantha. Pam
had a baby girl, Melanie the same week. Here we
were worried that we didn't have any grand kids! All
the girls are growing up just fine. They are delightful
to us. Jane and Gary's marriage didn't last so they
divorced. Later she married Tim Yates. Tim has a
boy, Bradley. They all live on Street Road, not far
from Peddlers Village.

Jane now works at the station. We would be lost
without her. She gets up at 5 a.m. and drives me to
dialysis, goes home, lets out her ducks and chickens
and then drives the girls to school, then comes to

work. She just can't do enough for us and how we appreciate it all. At this very moment, Tim is installing a new shower in our upstairs bath and doing a beautiful job.

TOM

Thomas Charles Melson, born July 13, 1969, was our fourth child and second son. You couldn't beat him at checkers. Like the others with all the lessons, he grew into a fine young man. Mt. Carmel, then LaSalle High School, then Clarion College where Uncle John lives. He then transferred to Temple. He loved football in high school. He played center, received an MVP award from all of the other coaches. Then he joined the Crew Team where he was center seat in the 8 man boat. He had several jobs but ended up at the station operating our emissions machine.

He shot his first deer with a black powder rifle. He bought a house in Doylestown, fixed it up, sold it and bought another house in Buckingham. He married

Coleen who has a daughter, Madison. They still live in Buckingham. They all went on a cruise where Tom caught a virus that really set him back. It has been over a year with slow recovery, but he's making it.

Ask him about his famous raccoon story...

TONY

Anthony Lewis Melson, born July 14, 1973. Tony is our third son and last child. Like the others, we tried to do everything that we could for him with lessons. Mt. Carmel, then we sent him to Solebury School. At graduation, he received the first and only award given by the school. That was quite an honor. Then he went to Delaware Valley College, got a job at Thriftway across the street from the station. Then he came to work at the station. In grade school he once won a TV for selling the most magazines in the whole school. He married a girl, Debbie and they bought a house in Colonial Greene in Doylestown. They have three beautiful kids, Jessica, Jack and Jill.

Tony is our one man band. He is our service manager, a notary along with Jane and is in charge of UHaul. He does a great job and puts in more hours than anybody.

He is a hunter, loves to hunt at Jimmy's. His first deer was a 6 point buck. He likes to do woodworking and has a pretty complete wood shop in his basement. He is also a good pool player. We would be lost without him. This past Christmas, Judy and I gave the station and property to all our kids. I am sure they will do well with it.

Pam and Jane both became First Class Girl Scouts. Jimmy and Tony both became Eagle Scouts. Tom loved football and was voted the MVP at LaSalle High School by all of the other coaches. He was also on an 8 man boat on the Crew Team.

JUDY

What can you say about someone that you have lived and loved almost your whole life? There just isn't enough words.

Judy was 15 when we started to date. I was 17. We did a lot of wonderful things together and had a wonderful life together. So it wasn't long before we started going steady. I remember coming home and I walked into our high school to see if I could find her. Our principal saw me, he was an old Navy man. Well he told me to go sit in my car. He then went and found her, brought her out and put her in my car and said take off and have fun. Do you think that would happen this day and age? No way.

Judy's mom wasn't thrilled about me at the time but she came around. Her dad was happy, it meant that he could hunt and trap on our farm. I became very fond of her folks and Donna, Kathy and John. It didn't take long before we were engaged.

I came home and we were married at St Martins. It was a small wedding, just family. Donna was maid of honor. Harry Hankins was my best man. My mom wouldn't come to our wedding. It really hurt. I never knew why. I took instructions in the Navy to become catholic! Which I did. My mom was protestant and my dad was catholic so I grew up without any religion. I wanted Judy and I to raise our kids in the same church. If it wasn't for Judy we would not have what we have today. I never told her this but she was the smartest person I ever knew and I would be lost without her. Even though she is a democrat and I am a republican, we always got along.

Judy is a wonderful mom to our kids and a wonderful cook. How did I get so lucky? I made her a recipe box and I put on it:

The way she looks
The way she cooks
is just delightful

She went right up the ladder being president of the Jr. Woman's Club and later President of the VIA. She became chairman of the board at Doylestown Hospital. She did an outstanding job at anything she did. Among other things she started the 1895 society. She finally retired from all that and just enjoys her quilt making and knitting things for all our grandkids.

I know she has reservations about being flooded out and that she is doing this for me. I wanted to move so in case I died she wouldn't have to go thru selling our house alone. If it does flood I am sure we can handle it together, with a lot of help from our kids not to mention Johnny and Kathy.

I couldn't live without her and wouldn't want to.

MY HOBBIES

I, like most people, go through different hobbies. I
guess my first one was hunting and gun collecting.
My friend Dave (Navy) got me into bow hunting
while we were in Florida and enjoyed it a lot. When
I got out of the Navy, archery was becoming very
popular. I started target shooting with my friends
Harry Getz and Big Joe Bradfield. Believe it or not
Joe shot a 125 pound bow when the rest of us used
50 pound bows. We would get together once a

week. Joe would always win. We used to keep track of how many arrows I shot. My bow string would break about 1,500 arrows. Then I started bow hunting for deer. What fun I had. I would only shoot at bucks. One year, I shot and missed 17 bucks. I don't know why but I just couldn't hit one. I had shot a ground hog and snakes but no deer. Next I got into rifles and would go to the mountains with my brother, Frank Soriero, Jay Petrie and his brother Kurt Petrie for the first 3 days of deer season. We usually bagged a couple. I have many good memories and stories. We all had Jeeps at the time.

The biggest buck I ever got was down the Cuttalosa it was a 7 pointer. One year, my friend Dave invited me to hunt in Georgia for deer and wild pigs. He came up from Florida and I came down from PA. He had a popup camper and we stayed at a camp ground on Fort Stewart. An Army base. The first day I got a 4 point buck. The second day I got 2 hogs with one shot. They just happened to stand next to one another. I was using my 3006 winchester and got them both. Those rebels are still talking about the yankee that got 2 hogs with one shot. I told them that is how we won the civil war.

I made a little blacksmith shop in our barnyard. Took a course and had a lot of fun making things out of steel.

I then got into woodworking. Made a workshop in part of the barn. A friend of Judy's husband started to teach me how to carve birds out of bass wood. I really enjoyed doing them and painting them. I made a ferris wheel with a bunch of birds that worked. I started to make bird houses. I think I made almost 100 of them and gave most away. I would make them to look like a person's home. I also started making all kinds of boxes and small chests. Even did some chip carving on some. I made a recipe box for Judy.

Peddlers Village had a bird house contest every year that I used to enter and I won a couple of blue ribbons.

VITA is an organization that helps people to learn to read and every year they hold an auction and one of my bird houses sold for $100. Not bad!!!!

I got interested in black powder and made my own left handed flint lock Kentucky rifle and shot a deer with it. We used to target shoot a lot of weekends. Even went to Canada hunting with my friend Ralph Horton and Judy's dad, Bud, for moose. Ralph was an outdoor writer and got Coleman company to sponsor our trip. They gave us everything that we needed for a camp out. Tent, sleeping bags, cots, stove and coolers. We had a nice trip but we didn't get anything.

I made a few powder horns and tried to scrimshaw them didn't turn out so good.

"Wrapping presents" is another organization that has a lot of members that make Christmas door decorations for nursing homes. So for the past couple of years I made a lot of them.

(Boxes dad handmade and painted for his Grandchildren)

I also took up painting. I took a couple art lessons with my friend Jay Petrie up at Prallsville Mill in Stockton, NJ. I loved it but with my eye problems I didn't do so well. My daughter Jane has some of my masterpieces. I think I pawned a few to all my kids, weather they liked them or not.

MY HEALTH

I have always considered myself to be in good shape until now.

I started with macular degeneration in my 40's and they have tried just about everything. It is the wet kind and a little rain. First in my right eye and later my left eye. It gave me a lot of problems with perception. But I was still able to read plus doing my hobbies, painting, woodworking. Even took some art lessons with my good friend Dr. Jay.

Over the years I've had a lot of laser surgeries, implants and injections into my eyes. At this point I am blind in my left eye but I can still read with my right eye. I just pray that I don't go completely blind before I die. I can't help but think that I am a real burden on my family. They have all been terrific putting up with me.

In 1991, I got a very rare thing called Ramsey Hunt syndrome. It looked like small pox with big sores only on half of your face around the hair line.

Also in 99, I had a thyroid problem which called for a 131 treatment. That was a radioactive pill I took. I went to the shore house, had to be away from everybody. I am not sure if I glowed in the dark or not.

In 1997, I had to have a stent implant for my heart. The funny thing was the doctor that did it was a boy scout in our troop.

In 1999, I had prostate surgery and they seemed to have gotten all the cancer.

My eye doctor was Dr. Steven Sinclair one of the best. Over the years he tried everything but to no avail. It just kept getting worse. I was getting a lot of severe headaches. He finally said that the eye had to come out. I couldn't see anything out of it anyway.

2011, I started with kidney failure. At one time as an experiment, I had to take 40 pills per day.

Of course all this time my kidneys were failing so in April 2011, I started dialysis treatments, 4 hours a day on Monday, Wednesday and Friday. It's been two years now. Without it I wouldn't be here writing this.

Around December 2012, I got bladder cancer and started treatments for 12 weeks which didn't work. Meanwhile I had to get a pacemaker put in to keep my heart under control. I also have to have a new fistula put into my arm for my dialysis treatments next week for that!!!

Two years ago, I bought Judy an IPAD for Christmas which I took over. It makes the time at dialysis go so quickly. I desired to try to write this story. I am not very good at it and I am sure I left a million things out but I did the best that I could.

February 27, 2013, left eye taken out.

March 6, 2013, pacemaker put in.

DAD'S LAST ENTRY

Now it's the middle of April and they can't seem to stop the bleeding in my bladder. I have been in and out of the hospital a dozen times with a lot of pain. So they are going to take out my bladder and both kidneys on Tuesday. It's a big operation, 7 to 8 hours with 4 doctors with a 1 to 2 week stay in the hospital. I have never been treated so kindly by everyone and I thank you all very much. You are all too kind.

If I don't make it, I want you to know that I have had a wonderful life and love you all with all my heart.

I know I can count on all of you to take care of Mom. She is the best thing that ever happened to me.

Don't cry because it's over SMILE because it happened.

DAD

ABOUT THE AUTHOR

James Pass Melson passed away on May 23, 2013 at home in New Hope surrounded by his family after a long battle with kidney failure and cancer. He was 78 years old. Jim was born on February 26, 1935 in Philadelphia, PA. His parents were Anna Pass Melson and Walter F. Melson of Watercress Springs, New Hope, PA. He spent his childhood in New Hope and graduated from New Hope Solebury High School where he met and married the love of his life, Judith Eichlin. A Korean War Veteran, he served in the United States Navy from 1953 to 1957 as a Flight Engineer.

If you were lucky enough to have known Jim, you were blessed. He poured his heart and soul into his business, Melson's Service Center which he began in 1966 in New Hope. He valued every customer who walked in the door. From Uhaul to Simplicity to selling gas and repairing cars, Jim enabled his business to thrive throughout the years. His children operate the "station" today.

At 17 years of age, he met his high school sweetheart, Judy who was 15 at the time. They married and raised their five children in Doylestown on Pine Run Farm and were lucky enough to live 56 years together. In 2012, they moved back home to New Hope to enjoy the magic of the "Glass House" and all it has to offer.

Nothing was impossible in Jim's eyes. He could do anything or figure out how to do it. During his life, Jim had many hobbies which included hunting, painting, and woodworking. His creativity was a gift that he used in every project he took on. He made many pieces of art including bird houses, walking sticks, hand carved wooden boxes and paintings that he gave to family and friends over the years. He wanted to give a piece of himself to everyone, and he did just that.

Pop Pop and Jack

After retirement, he enjoyed being a volunteer at the Delaware Valley Historical Aircraft Association's Wings of Freedom Aviation Museum. He was also a life member of the American Legion Post 79 in New

Hope. As a father, he always made time for every project, activity or Scouting event that his children had. He will be forever missed.

Jim was pre-deceased by his brother, Walter F. Melson, Jr. and his sisters, Marie Jane Melson Heath and Marlene E. He is survived by his wife, Judy and their five children, Pam Melson-Abele, James Jr (Ellen), Jane Melson Yates (Timothy), Thomas Melson (Coleen) and Anthony Melson (Deborah) along with their 10 Grandchildren, Jennifer, Melanie, Madison, Grace, Samantha, Cary, Bradley, Jessica, Jack, Jill and many nieces and nephews.

A GOOD MAN

"Don't cry because it's over, smile because it happened". Several times Jim said this to me. He even wrote it as his own final farewell words. I think he found reflective peace in this thought, but knowing Jim, thinking of others, he shared this thought in the hope it would ease their pain upon his passing.

So, why should there be smiles because James Melson happened? How long do I have?

His family, he and his wife, Judith, were together and inseparable for over 60 years. He was 17 when they started dating, and Judy was 15. Together they raised five children – Pamela, James Jr., Jane, Thomas and Anthony. They have ten grandchildren. Jim dearly loved his family. He loved being surrounded by them. After moving to Pine Run Farm, the family converted the cow stalls in the barn into a recreation room. In deciding where to locate his wood shop, Jim chose the corner of the rec room, instead of the former separate milk parlor, which would have been more suitable. Why? Because he wanted to be near so as to see his family as he worked. There was never a "man cave" for Jim.

His friends, Jim's circle of friends was wide and reached back to his childhood. His social nature fostered friendships. Friendships that endured throughout the years. From school years, beginning at the one room school house in Solebury, to the years in the United States Navy, during the Korean War, to his years in business as Melson's Service Center, to his association in the American Legion, to his years in retirement when he volunteered at the Air Museum, and finally to his time during medical rehabilitation. Being Jim's friend was special indeed.

His intellect, knowledge and skills, Jim had a gifted mind. He was curious and creative, inquisitive and imaginative. His mind was always working, even up to the last. He thrived on the challenges that problems presented. Ever since I can remember, I marveled at this. He would ponder the problem, and with his knowledge and mechanical skills, effect the best solution. Every semester, in teaching my students law, I used Jim as an example of a master problem solver. That is, the use of the same process of intellect, knowledge and skills, that are essential in any successful profession or trade.

In addition to being blessed with this gift, Jim was incredibly industrious. As a result, he created in 1966 a business, Melson's Service Center, of which he was rightly proud. Because of Jim, the business thrived and prospered to the point that his children now carry it on. Knowing that his family, possibly future generations of his family, will continue to carry it on made him extremely happy.

His character – I want you to think. Think of all your memories of Jim. I am certain you are all like me. In my memories, all I see is a good, kind, gentle, caring, and giving person. I never saw or knew of any anger or rage, any hatred, any selfishness, or greed – ever. Judy shared this story with me. Jim began dialysis two years ago. The center opened at 6:00 a.m., and three times per week, Jane drove him there. The first time he arrived, Jim, not knowing the protocol, walked to the locked door, in front of which there was a line. When the door opened, he held the door for all of those in line to go before him. He continued to do this every time that he went. That is who he was – always thinking of others, enriching the lives of others, making life better for others.

He was happy when he arrived home from the hospital. He was so happy to be visited and surrounded by his loved ones. And Jim, always thinking, always considerate, whispered to Judy, "This might sound crazy, but why don't you get a guest book."

Please share your memories of Jim Melson to others. Those memories will always be with us until our end. Jim Melson's life was a good life, one of which the world needs more. His life deserves to be remembered for a long, long time.

"Don't cry because it's over, smile because it happened." With Jim's permission, I would like to change that a bit – "Do cry because it's over and do smile because it happened."

With love,

John Eichlin

Made in the USA
Columbia, SC
27 June 2017